365 Insightful Questions for Boys Aged 13-14

365
Insightful Questions
for Boys Aged 13-14

One Question a Day for Personal Growth and Confidence Building

Aria Capri Publishing
Devon Abbruzzese
Mauricio Vasquez

Toronto, Canada

365 Insightful Questions for Boys Aged 13-14 by Aria Capri Publishing [Aria Capri International Inc.]. All Rights Reserved.

Authors:
Devon Abbruzzese
Mauricio Vasquez
Aria Capri Publishing

First Printing: May 2024

ISBN-978-1-998402-37-3 (Paperback book)
ISBN-978-1-998402-36-6 (Hardcover book)
ISBN-978-1-998402-35-9 (Electronic book)

Introduction

Welcome to a journey that is as critical as it is transformative, a journey through the crucial years of early adolescence. This book is dedicated to fostering a deeper understanding of boys aged 13 to 14—a transformative stage where young teens begin to navigate the complex pathways of identity, relationships, and personal growth. Here, we embark on an exploration of the vital role that thoughtful, probing questions play in engaging and developing the adolescent mind and spirit.

The Power of Questions

At the heart of this guide is a profound yet simple tool: the question. Questions are the keys that unlock the inner workings of the adolescent mind, revealing thoughts, feelings, and perceptions that even they might not yet fully understand. By encouraging boys to articulate their views, we provide them with a framework to explore their identities and the world around them. Questions serve not just to gather information but to validate the experiences and emotions of these young individuals, affirming their worth and their place in the world.

Why Questions Matter

Boys experience rapid physical, emotional, and intellectual growth during early adolescence. As their bodies and minds develop, so does their need for deeper understanding and connection. Questions tailored to their experiences encourage reflection and critical thinking, promote emotional intelligence, and foster a sense of competency and autonomy.

However, the benefits of engaging adolescents with meaningful questions extend far beyond the individual. These interactions are invaluable for parents, educators, and mentors. They offer insights into a boy's inner life, helping adults provide better support, guidance, and encouragement. Moreover, these dialogues build trust and strengthen relationships, creating a foundation of mutual respect and understanding that supports healthy development.

Transformative Interactions

Each question posed in this book is designed to challenge, inspire, and motivate young adolescents to connect with both their internal and external worlds. Through these questions, boys are encouraged to:
- Reflect on their personal values and beliefs.
- Articulate their feelings and manage their emotions.
- Develop stronger relationships with peers and family members.
- Enhance their problem-solving and critical thinking skills.

This process is not about finding the "right" answers. Instead, it's about the exploration and asking the right questions that prompt boys to consider their place in the world and their connections to others. Such explorations are crucial at a stage when adolescents are defining who they are and who they aspire to be.

A Call to Engage

As you progress through this book, each chapter will introduce a different aspect of adolescent life—ranging from physical and emotional development to social interactions and educational challenges. The questions provided are crafted to spark meaningful, relevant, engaging discussions for boys navigating these complex years. They are designed to be flexible, allowing for adaptation based on each adolescent's unique personality and circumstances.

This book aims to be more than just a resource—it seeks to be a companion. A companion that understands the challenges and joys of raising and interacting with young adolescents. As we delve into the questions guiding the coming year, remember that the ultimate goal is to empower these young individuals to become thoughtful, confident, and caring adults.

By embracing the power of questions, we can transform everyday interactions with our boys into profound opportunities for growth and connection. Let us commit to asking not just any questions, but the right questions—ones that challenge, inspire, and lead to greater understanding and empathy.

Let the journey of questions begin.

Devon & Mauricio

Share Your Experience

Thank you for choosing this book. We hope this has provided meaningful insights and fostered valuable conversations for you and your child.

Your feedback helps us improve and helps other parents and young readers discover this resource. Reviews increase the book's visibility, making it easier for those who might benefit from its content to find it.

If you found this book helpful, please take a moment to leave a review by scanning this QR code.

Your experience can inspire and guide others on their journey of self-discovery and growth. We appreciate your support. Thank you.

Devon & Mauricio

Scan the QR code to access the full collection

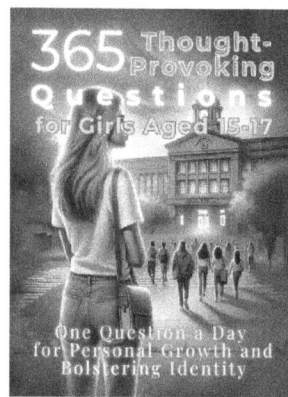

Disclaimer

Dear Readers,

This book is designed to serve as a tool for personal growth, reflection, and exploring thoughts and feelings. The questions provided within these pages aim to inspire introspection and conversation, fostering a deeper understanding of oneself and the world.

However, it is important to understand that this book is not a substitute for professional advice, diagnosis, or treatment. While the questions can guide meaningful discussions and self-discovery, they are not intended to address or resolve serious issues or health concerns.

If you or your child encounters significant emotional, psychological, or physical challenges, we strongly recommend seeking the guidance of a qualified professional. This may include consulting a doctor, mental health professional, counselor, or any other relevant specialist who can provide the appropriate support and interventions.

The publisher, author, and any associated parties take no responsibility for any consequences resulting from the use of this book. It is up to the reader to exercise their judgment and discretion when engaging with the questions and interpreting their answers. The insights and reflections gained from this book should be seen as a starting point for further exploration and, when necessary, professional consultation.

We hope that this book serves as a valuable resource for personal growth and development. Remember, each individual's journey of self-discovery is unique, and seeking help when needed is a sign of strength and wisdom.

Guidelines for Asking Questions to Adolescents

Read the following guidelines to learn more about asking questions that unlock learning, foster communication and improve relationships.

- **Effective questions are open or focused, depending on the context**: Questions that open awareness and learning are open-ended questions that cannot be answered with a yes or no. Such questions evoke deeper thinking and reflection.

- **Effective questions support learning**: The goal is to stimulate thinking and deepen understanding of the situation. Insightful questions should focus on the most valuable aspects of the issue at hand, helping adolescents better understand their experiences and feelings.

- **Effective questions are asked for the benefit of others**. The intent is to stimulate adolescents' thinking and deepen their understanding. It is not necessarily about the questioner and their needs.

- **Effective questions engage a personal response**: Engaging adolescents by inviting a personal response—how they feel, what emotions they are bringing to the situation—is crucial. The more a question invites a personal response to a challenge or choice, the more powerful it is for facilitating learning and growth.

- **Effective questions look beyond problems to future outcomes**: When adolescents are entangled in a problem, impactful questions shift the perspective from the problem to the solution, opening new opportunities for action and positive thinking.

- **Effective questions facilitate openness versus defensiveness**: Impactful questions are worded and expressed with a non-judgmental tone and open body language to prevent a defensive reaction. It is usually best to avoid questions that begin with "why" since they often elicit defensive responses or explanations.

- **Effective questions co-create best options versus manipulating outcomes**: Impactful questions are not intended to manipulate or lead adolescents to the option you might think is the best. If you want to suggest, it is best made directly as a suggestion versus a disguised directive through a question.

- **Less is more**: For questions, less is usually more. Ask only one question at a time and avoid long-winded, complicated questions.

Day 1

What physical activity do you enjoy the most, and how does it make you feel afterward?

Day 2

Can you describe a time when you felt really proud of yourself? What did you do?

Day 3

What qualities do you look for in a friend, and why are these important to you?

Day 4

When learning something new, do you prefer to read, watch, or do something hands-on? Why?

Day 5
What is one skill you've learned this year that you think will be useful for the rest of your life?

Day 6
What do you do when you feel stressed or overwhelmed?

Day 7
Which family tradition do you value the most and why?

Day 8
What does feeling safe mean to you?

Day 9
Do you think it's more important to be fair or to be kind? Can you explain your choice?

Day 10
If you could choose, would you prefer living in a city or the countryside? What's your reasoning?

Day 11
What is your favorite healthy meal, and why do you like it?

Day 12
What is one question you have about changes happening to your body during puberty?

Day 13
What are three words you would use to describe yourself, and why?

Day 14
How do you calm down when you're feeling really angry?

Day 15
Can you think of a time when you really understood how someone else was feeling? What happened?

Day 16
What do you think makes a friendship strong?

Day 17
What's something fun you like doing with your family?

Day 18
How do you decide what to share on social media?

Day 19
What's a problem you've solved recently, and how did you do it?

Day 20
What book have you read that you would recommend to a friend? Why?

Day 21
Do you think everyone learns in the same way? Why or why not?

Day 22
What's something new you've learned this school year that surprised you?

Day 23
What is your favorite word, and what does it mean?

Day 24
When was the last time you made a new friend, and how did it happen?

Day 25
What makes you feel anxious, and how do you cope with that feeling?

Day 26
Can you share a time when you had to overcome a big challenge?

Day 27
Why do you think it's important to talk about our feelings and mental health?

Day 28
How does your cultural background influence your daily life?

Day 29
What is something you saw in a movie or on TV that you want to try in real life?

Day 30
How do you think where we live affects how we live?

Day 31
What's one rule at home or school that helps keep you safe?

Day 32
What do you need to feel supported when you're upset?

Day 33
What's the most important rule you follow when online to stay safe?

Day 34
Is there ever a time when it's okay to break a rule? Can you explain?

Day 35
What are some questions you have about life or the universe?

Day 36
What's your favorite outdoor activity and why?

Day 37
Do you think kids grow up differently in urban areas compared to rural areas? In what ways?

Day 38
How do you think your eating habits affect your mood and energy levels?

Day 39
If you could try any new sport or physical activity, what would it be and why?

Day 40
What is one thing you wish adults understood about what it's like to be a teenager today?

Day 41

What do you like most about yourself and why?

Day 42

What song always makes you feel better when you're upset?

Day 43

Who is someone you admire for how they handle their emotions, and what can you learn from them?

Day 44

How do you handle disagreements with your friends?

Day 45
What's something you appreciate about each member of your family?

Day 46
How do you feel social media affects your friendships?

Day 47
What kind of puzzles or games do you find challenging and enjoyable?

Day 48
Can you think of a math skill that you use in everyday life? How do you use it?

Day 49
What is your favorite way to learn new things, and how does it help you?

Day 50
Can you describe a recent time when you figured out a solution to a difficult problem?

Day 51
What new word did you learn this month, and what does it mean?

Day 52
Describe a time when you helped a friend feel better. What did you do?

Day 53
What are three things that can help you relax when you feel tense?

Day 54
When something doesn't go your way, what's something positive you tell yourself?

Day 55
Why do you think it's important for people to understand mental health issues?

Day 56
How do the values of your culture affect the way you see the world?

Day 57
What's something you learned from the media that influenced a decision you made?

Day 58
Do you think your community has enough resources for kids your age? What would you add?

Day 59
What do you do to make sure you stay safe when you're playing outside?

Day 60
What does a supportive environment at school look like for you?

Day 61
What advice would you give someone younger about staying safe online?

Day 62
What does 'doing the right thing' mean to you daily?

Day 63
What are some ways you find meaning or purpose in your life?

Day 64
How does spending time outside influence your mood and thoughts?

Day 65
What are the pros and cons of growing up in your specific community?

Day 66
What changes have you noticed in your strength or stamina over the last year?

Day 67
Can you describe a recent situation where you had to manage difficult Emotions?

Day 68
What do you think is the biggest challenge about making new friends?

Day 69
What subject in school do you find most challenging, and what strategies help you in studying it?

Day 70
What personal achievement are you most proud of this year?

Day 71
What activities make you feel happiest and most at peace?

Day 72
How do you think your culture shapes your views on what careers or hobbies you should pursue?

Day 73
Have you ever felt unsafe online? What did you do about it?

Day 74
What values are most important to you, and how do you try to live by them?

Day 75
What environmental issue concerns you the most, and why?

Day 76
How has your height changed in the past year, and how do you feel about it?

Day 77
What is something new you've tried recently that made you feel happy?

Day 78
How do you usually handle situations when you and a friend disagree on something?

Day 79
What's a subject you think will help you most in your future career? Why?

Day 80
Can you think of a new hobby you'd like to explore this year? What attracts you to it?

Day 81
What's your strategy for dealing with homework that you find difficult or frustrating?

Day 82
Who in your life do you think understands you the best?

Day 83
What sport do you enjoy watching, and what do you learn from it?

Day 84
What was the most interesting thing you learned this week?

Day 85
Do you prefer team sports or individual sports, and why?

Day 86
What is one thing you do that helps you relax after a stressful day?

Day 87
What's one thing you admire about your best friend?

Day 88
What was the last book you read, and what did you think about it?

Day 89
Have you ever helped someone with a problem? What did you do?

Day 90
What is something you're looking forward to in the next month?

Day 91
How do you feel technology impacts your daily life?

Day 92
What's one goal you have for this school year?

Day 93
Describe a time when you felt very courageous. What were you doing?

Day 94
What's your favorite memory from the past year?

Day 95
If you could learn any skill instantly, what would it be and why?

Day 96
What's something you've learned about managing your time and tasks effectively?

Day 97
When was the last time you tried something new, and what was it?

Day 98
What do you think makes a good leader?

Day 99
How do you decide if you trust someone?

Day 100
What's one way you've changed in the last year that you're proud of?

Day 101
Who is someone you look up to, and what qualities do they have that you admire?

Day 102
What's the most important lesson you've learned from your parents?

Day 103
How do you deal with feelings of anger or frustration?

Day 104
What's your favorite way to spend a weekend, and why?

Day 105
Describe a dream you have for your future. What does it involve?

Day 106
What does friendship mean to you?

Day 107
What subject in school do you find most useful, and why?

Day 108
What's one piece of advice you would give to a younger child?

Day 109
What are three things you do well?

Day 110
How do you approach making new friends?

Day 111
When do you feel the most confident?

Day 112
What does a perfect day look like to you?

Day 113
What's one thing you could teach someone else to do?

Day 114
How do you handle it when someone disagrees with your opinion?

Day 115
What's a recent good deed you've done?

Day 116
Describe your favorite place in the world and why it means so much to you.

Day 117
What song best represents your life right now, and why?

Day 118
What's the best advice you've ever received?

Day 119
What do you do to cheer yourself up when you're sad?

Day 120
What's something you hope to learn in the next year?

Day 121
What's your favorite family tradition?

Day 122
Who is your favorite fictional character, and what do you admire about them?

Day 123
What are three things you're grateful for today?

Day 124
What skills do you think are important to have in life?

Day 125
What's a challenge you've overcome that made you feel proud?

Day 126
What do you think is the most interesting thing about space or the universe?

Day 127
What new activity or hobby would you like to try, and why?

Day 128
What's something you've done that was outside of your comfort zone?

Day 129
What do you appreciate most about your culture?

Day 130
How do you think being a teenager today is different from when your parents were teens?

Day 131
What's your favorite way to express yourself creatively?

Day 132
How do you think money impacts people's lives?

Day 133
What's one world problem you wish you could solve?

Day 134
How do you make decisions about what is right and wrong?

Day 135
What are your thoughts on honesty? When is it hard to be honest?

Day 136
What's the most interesting piece of technology you use?

Day 137
What does leadership mean to you, and do you see yourself as a leader?

Day 138
How do you deal with changes, especially those you did not expect?

Day 139
What book significantly influenced your thinking?

Day 140
What are your thoughts on teamwork in sports and in school?

Day 141
What makes you unique from your friends?

Day 142
How do you like to celebrate your achievements?

Day 143
What's one thing you wish adults understood better about teenagers?

Day 144
How do you balance your time between school, hobbies, and friends?

Day 145
What are your strategies for dealing with bullying or negative peer pressure?

Day 146
How important is privacy to you, especially online?

Day 147
What's a scientific fact that fascinates you?

Day 148
How do you feel about your future? What excites or worries you?

Day 149
What does being a good citizen mean to you?

Day 150
What's one way you help out at home?

Day 151
What was a moment this year when you felt most connected to your family?

Day 152
How do you think future technologies will change how we learn at school?

Day 153
When was a time you helped a stranger? How did that make you feel?

Day 154
What's your favorite outdoor activity, and why do you enjoy it?

Day 155
How does music affect your mood and emotions?

Day 156
What's the bravest thing you've ever done?

Day 157
What qualities make a good teacher or mentor?

Day 158
What's one thing you'd like to change about your daily routine?

Day 159
What do you value most in your friendships?

Day 160
What's a new skill you'd like to master, and why?

Day 161
How do you think traveling to different places can affect a person?

Day 162
What's a local issue in your community that you care about?

Day 163
Describe a time when you had to work hard to achieve something.

Day 164
What does 'family' mean to you?

Day 165
What's your biggest goal for the next school year?

Day 166
What would you do if you were president of your country for a day?

Day 167
How do you feel about public speaking, and what could make it easier for you?

Day 168
What's a science fact that blows your mind?

Day 169
How do you react when you encounter something new or unfamiliar?

Day 170
What's one habit you would like to develop this year?

Day 171
How do you express gratitude to others?

Day 172
What's your favorite game to play with friends and why?

Day 173
What's one thing you've learned about your health this year?

Day 174
How do you decide what's fair in a disagreement?

Day 175
What's something you're curious about learning more deeply?

Day 176
How does being in nature make you feel?

Day 177
What role does technology play in your relationships?

Day 178
What's the most important lesson you've learned from a movie or book?

Day 179
How do you prioritize your activities and tasks?

Day 180
What's something you've done that made you feel extremely proud?

Day 181
How do you approach learning a new skill or subject?

Day 182
What's a global issue that you think more people should be aware of?

Day 183
How do you maintain a healthy balance between schoolwork and free time?

Day 184
What do you find most rewarding about your favorite hobby?

Day 185
What's something you admire about your parents or guardians?

Day 186
What's your favorite thing about your hometown?

Day 187
Describe a time when you had to show resilience.

Day 188
What kind of books do you like to read, and why?

Day 189
How do you feel about your personal safety in your community?

Day 190
What's something new you'd like to try this summer?

Day 191
Who is someone in your life who makes you feel heard and understood?

Day 192
What's a new technology you wish could be invented?

Day 193
How do you react when you face a big challenge?

Day 194
What do you think are the most important qualities in a leader?

Day 195
What's a topic you'd like to know more about?

Day 196
How do you handle conflicts with your peers?

Day 197
What are your thoughts on teamwork in school projects?

Day 198
What's something you feel passionate about and why?

Day 199
How do you prepare for a test or a big project?

Day 200
What's one way you've helped your community?

Day 201
How do you feel when you try something new?

Day 202
What's your strategy for managing stress before a big event, like a sports game or exam?

Day 203
What's the funniest thing that happened to you recently?

Day 204
What's something you've done that you never thought you could do?

<u>Day 205</u>
What's the best way to make new friends, in your opinion?

<u>Day 206</u>
What does being healthy mean to you?

<u>Day 207</u>
What's the most interesting piece of art you've seen? What did you like about it?

<u>Day 208</u>
How do you decide what is right and wrong?

Day 209
What's a goal you have for the next year?

Day 210
How do you like to celebrate your personal achievements?

Day 211
What's your favorite thing about yourself?

Day 212
What's one thing you could teach someone else?

Day 213
What's your favorite season, and why?

Day 214
What qualities do you admire in others?

Day 215
How do you deal with disappointment?

Day 216
What's something you're looking forward to in the next month?

Day 217
How do you like to spend time outdoors?

Day 218
What's a recent dream you had that you remember?

Day 219
What's something new you'd like to learn how to do?

Day 220
What's something you've done that made you feel very brave?

Day 221
What's the best advice you've ever given someone?

Day 222
What does friendship mean to you?

Day 223
How do you deal with changes at school or home?

Day 224
What's a skill you'd like to improve?

<u>Day 225</u>
What's your favorite family activity?

<u>Day 226</u>
What makes you feel peaceful?

<u>Day 227</u>
How do you help out at home?

<u>Day 228</u>
What's a subject you wish was taught in school?

Day 229
What's the most useful thing you've learned from someone younger than you?

Day 230
What do you think makes a good friend?

Day 231
What's something you've learned about your family history that you find interesting?

Day 232
How do you motivate yourself to do schoolwork?

Day 233
What's something you admire about your culture?

Day 234
What are your strategies for making new friends?

Day 235
What hobbies would you like to explore next year?

Day 236
What's a personal challenge you've overcome recently?

Day 237
How do you think you've changed in the past year?

Day 238
What's your favorite way to relax after a long day?

Day 239
What's a book or movie that had a big impact on you?

Day 240
What's one thing you want to accomplish before you finish school?

Day 241
What are you most grateful for in your life right now?

Day 242
How do you like to unwind at the end of a busy day?

Day 243
What's a big goal you hope to achieve in the next five years?

Day 244
What kind of volunteer work would you be interested in doing?

Day 245
What does loyalty mean to you in friendships?

Day 246
What's the most important lesson you've learned from a family member?

Day 247
If you could invent something, what would it be and why?

Day 248
What's your favorite way to express yourself artistically?

Day 249
How do you think being a teenager today is different from when your parents were teens?

Day 250
What do you think is the best way to resolve conflicts with others?

Day 251
What book has influenced you the most, and why?

Day 252
How do you approach making difficult decisions?

Day 253
What makes you feel truly alive and excited?

Day 254
What is something you've done that required a lot of courage?

Day 255
How do you prepare for an important test or presentation?

Day 256
What's your favorite family memory?

Day 257
What traits do you admire most in others?

Day 258
What new skill would you like to learn this year, and why?

Day 259
What's your favorite sport to play, and what do you enjoy about it?

Day 260
How do you handle peer pressure?

Day 261
What's something new you'd like to try that you've never done before?

Day 262
How do you contribute to your family or community?

Day 263
What do you do when you feel overwhelmed by school or responsibilities?

Day 264
What's one change you'd like to make to your daily routine?

Day 265
What do you think is your strongest quality?

Day 266
What's something you believe that other people might disagree with?

Day 267
How do you stay focused when you have a lot of tasks to complete?

Day 268
What's your favorite quote or saying, and why does it resonate with you?

Day 269
What's one way you've changed in the past year that makes you proud?

Day 270
How do you approach learning about a topic you know nothing about?

Day 271
What do you appreciate most about your school?

Day 272
What's your strategy for dealing with setbacks?

Day 273
How do you express gratitude towards others?

Day 274
What's one hobby you think could become a passion of yours?

Day 275
What's the kindest thing someone has done for you?

Day 276
How do you decide what activities to prioritize in your free time?

Day 277
What does friendship mean to you, and how do you show a friend that they are important to you?

Day 278
What's the most challenging aspect of school for you?

Day 279
What historical figure do you admire, and why?

Day 280
How do you keep yourself motivated when tasks become challenging?

Day 281
What's a personal value you refuse to compromise on?

Day 282
What's a recent act of kindness you've witnessed or performed?

Day 283
What's one thing you've learned about yourself through a difficult time?

Day 284
What's your favorite place to think and reflect?

Day 285
How do you handle criticism from others?

Day 286
What's a tradition you cherish in your family?

Day 287
What role does technology play in your life?

Day 288
What's one lesson you've learned from a mistake you made?

Day 289
What are your thoughts on leadership? What makes someone a good leader?

Day 290
What's one area of your life where you'd like to see improvement?

Day 291
How do you celebrate your achievements?

Day 292
What does success mean to you?

Day 293
What's a recent challenge you overcame, and how did you do it?

Day 294
What's something you'd like to learn about your cultural heritage?

Day 295
How do you make time for yourself?

Day 296
What's one piece of advice you would give to someone younger than you?

Day 297
What do you think is the most interesting part of learning a new language?

Day 298
What's something you do to help take care of the environment?

Day 299
How do you balance school and leisure?

Day 300
What's your favorite memory from the past year?

Day 301
What's a fear you've faced, and how did you overcome it?

Day 302
What inspires you to learn?

Day 303
How do you think about the future? What do you hope to achieve?

Day 304
What are the most important lessons you've learned from sports or other extracurricular activities?

Day 305
How do you think your friends would describe you?

Day 306
What's one thing you're exceptionally good at?

Day 307
How do you handle feeling nervous or anxious?

Day 308
What's one way you've grown that you never expected?

Day 309
What's something new you'd like to learn in school?

Day 310
What's something creative you've done that you're proud of?

Day 311
How do you feel about taking on new responsibilities?

Day 312
What are you most curious about right now?

Day 313
How do you think your hobbies influence your personality?

Day 314
What do you appreciate most about your best friend?

Day 315
What's a recent positive change you've noticed about yourself?

Day 316
How do you cope with disappointment or setbacks?

Day 317
What new skill would you like to develop next year, and why?

Day 318
What's your favorite tradition or holiday, and what makes it special?

Day 319
How do you contribute to your school or local community?

Day 320
What's a subject you feel passionate about and wish others knew more about?

Day 321
How do you handle situations where you have to work with someone you don't get along with?

Day 322
What's the best way to start your day, in your opinion?

Day 323
Who in your life gives you the best advice, and what was the last great piece they shared with you?

Day 324
How do you balance your time between technology and outdoor activities?

Day 325
What's one thing you've learned from a movie or TV show that stuck with you?

Day 326
What's an important lesson you've learned from playing sports?

Day 327
How do you make sure you're listening to others when they're speaking to you?

Day 328
What's a personal goal you've set for yourself this month?

Day 329
How do you show someone you care about them?

Day 330
What's a book that has inspired you, and why?

Day 331
What do you think makes a good teammate or friend?

Day 332
How do you approach solving a problem at school or home?

Day 333
What's something you've done that you initially thought you couldn't do?

Day 334
How do you prepare for a big event or test?

Day 335
What's one thing you'd like to change about your daily routine?

Day 336
How do you decide what's important when you have multiple priorities?

Day 337
What do you do to stay healthy and active?

Day 338
How do you express your creativity?

Day 339
What's something you admire about a teacher or coach, and why?

Day 340
What's the most interesting project you've worked on recently?

Day 341
How do you deal with feelings of anxiety or stress?

Day 342
What are your strategies for learning something difficult?

Day 343
How do you like to celebrate your successes?

Day 344
What's a place you've visited that made a significant impact on you?

Day 345
How do you think your actions affect others?

Day 346
What's something you do to help relax and unwind?

Day 347
How do you approach making new friends?

Day 348
What's the most useful piece of advice you've ever received?

Day 349
What's something you're looking forward to learning in school?

Day 350
How do you think people can make a positive difference in their communities?

Day 351
What's a challenge you recently faced and how did you handle it?

Day 352
How do you think respect is earned?

Day 353
What's the most memorable conversation you've had this year?

Day 354
How do you make decisions about what's right and wrong?

Day 355
What are your thoughts on leadership and being a leader?

Day 356
How do you handle mistakes, both yours and others'?

Day 357
What's something new you'd like to try in the upcoming year?

Day 358
How do you prioritize your mental health?

Day 359
What's a hobby you would recommend to a friend, and why?

Day 360
What do you think is the key to a happy life?

Day 361
How do you find motivation when you feel like giving up?

Day 362
What's one way you've helped someone else this year?

Day 363
How do you celebrate your cultural heritage?

Day 364
What's the most important thing you've learned from your parents?

Day 365
Reflecting on this past year, what are you most proud of achieving?

<u>Share Your Experience</u>

Thank you for choosing this book. We hope this has provided meaningful insights and fostered valuable conversations for you and your child.

Your feedback helps us improve and helps other parents and young readers discover this resource. Reviews increase the book's visibility, making it easier for those who might benefit from its content to find it.

If you found this book helpful, please take a moment to leave a review by scanning this QR code.

Your experience can inspire and guide others on their journey of self-discovery and growth. We appreciate your support. Thank you.

Devon & Mauricio